soups

soups

Alexandria, Virginia

Time-Life Books is a division of Time Life Inc.

TIME LIFE INC.

Chairman and CEO	Jim Nelson
President and COO	Steven L. Janas

TIME-LIFE TRADE PUBLISHING

Vice President and Publisher	Neil Levin
Senior Director of Acquisitions and Editorial Resources	Jennifer Pearce
Director of New Product Development	Carolyn Clark
Director of Marketing	Inger Forland
Director of Trade Sales	Dana Hobson
Director of Custom Publishing	John Lalor
Director of Special Markets	Robert Lombardi
Director of Design	Kate L. McConnell

SOUPS

Project Manager	Jennie Halfant
Technical Specialist	Monika Lynde

This edition first published in the U.K. in 1999 by Hamlyn
Octopus Publishing Group Limited
2–4 Heron Quays
London E14 4JP

Printed in China
10 9 8 7 6 5 4 3 2 1

Library of Congress Cataloging-in-Publication Data
Soups: over 60 simple recipes for elegant home cooking.
p. cm.
Includes index.
ISBN 0-7370-2057-1
1. Soups.

TX757 .S63595 2000
641.8'13--dc21

00-023455

Notes

1 Milk should be whole milk unless otherwise stated.

2 Fresh herbs should be used unless otherwise stated. If unavailable, use dried herbs as an alternative but only half the amount stated.

3 Pepper should be freshly ground black pepper unless otherwise stated; season according to taste.

4 Do not refreeze a dish that has been frozen previously.

contents

introduction

Soup is an amazingly versatile dish. While nothing is more welcome than a hearty vegetable broth on a cold winter's evening, a delicately flavored chilled soup makes a deliciously refreshing summer lunch. Creamy soups have a sophisticated richness of flavor that makes them perfect for a dinner party.

Making soup is surprisingly easy. It is always worth buying the best quality ingredients and using a good stock. Fresh herbs are always preferable to dried. Use a large, heavy pot so that the ingredients do not stick to the bottom and there is plenty of room to stir the soup. Serve hot soup in a warmed tureen or warmed bowls. Chill the bowls for serving iced soups.

Stock

Although bouillon cubes may be satisfactory and convenient for some types of dishes, a good-quality stock is essential for really successful soup. The flavor is incomparable and you are in control of the seasoning—most bouillon cubes tend to be quite salty. The ingredients for stock are inexpensive and it is very easy to make. Chicken necks and bones for stock are often available at supermarkets or can be bought at a meat market. Fish trimmings are also available and, if you are buying fresh fish from a fish market, always ask for the head and the trimmings from the fish to be filleted, and use them for making stock.

Four stock recipes follow and these form the basis of almost all the recipes in this book. Beef stock is a rich brown color and is ideal for meaty soups and those made with strongly flavored vegetables. It requires long, slow cooking, but is worth it. Chicken stock, which can be made from raw trimmings or the carcass of a cooked chicken, is a good all-purpose stock. Fish stock is quite delicately flavored and very quickly made. It is ideal for fish and seafood soups, although chicken stock may be substituted. Vegetable stock is quite light and is perfect for aromatic vegetable soups. You can use virtually any vegetables you like, but avoid floury root vegetables, such as potatoes, as they will make the stock cloudy. Add tomatoes for extra richness and a sliver of orange or lemon rind for an extra lift.

Never try to hurry stock. It needs to simmer very gently or it will evaporate too quickly. Do not add salt to the stock because as it reduces, the flavors concentrate and it might become too salty. Season with salt when making the soup. Always remove the scum that rises to the surface using a skimmer or slotted spoon. Once it is cooked, strain the stock—ideally, through a cheesecloth-lined strainer—and allow it to cool completely before storing in the refrigerator. A layer of fat will usually form on the surface of cold beef and chicken stock. Remove and discard this before using. All stocks freeze well. You can store them in plastic tubs or freeze them in ice cube trays and then pack in freezer bags for ease of storage.

beef stock

1 Put the bones in a roasting pan and cook in a preheated oven, 450°F, for about 1 hour, or until just browned and the fat and juices have run out. Using a slotted spoon, transfer the bones to a large pot.

2 Place the roasting pan over a low heat. Add the onions, carrots, and celery and fry, stirring frequently, for 10 minutes, or until browned. Transfer the vegetables to the pot, together with the bay leaves, parsley, thyme, and peppercorns. Pour in the water.

3 Bring to a boil and skim off any scum that rises to the surface. Lower the heat and simmer, skimming the surface occasionally, for 8 hours. Strain. Chill in the refrigerator. Remove any fat from the surface before using.

5 lb. beef bones or beef and veal bones

2 onions, roughly chopped

2 carrots, roughly chopped

2 celery stalks, roughly chopped

2 bay leaves

3–4 parsley sprigs

2 thyme sprigs

10 black peppercorns

5 quarts cold water

Makes about 3 quarts

Preparation time: 5–10 minutes

Cooking time: about 9 hours

chicken stock

1 Chop the chicken carcass into 3–4 pieces and place in a large pot, together with the giblets and trimmings. Add the carrots, onion, celery, herbs, and water, and bring to a boil, skimming off any scum that rises to the surface.

2 Lower the heat and simmer, skimming the surface occasionally, for 2–2½ hours. Strain through a cheesecloth-lined strainer. Store in the refrigerator.

cooked chicken carcass plus raw giblets and trimmings

2 large carrots, roughly chopped

1 onion, roughly chopped

1 celery stalk, roughly chopped

1 thyme sprig

1 bay leaf

4–6 parsley sprigs, lightly crushed

2 quarts cold water

Makes about 1 quart

Preparation time: 5–10 minutes

Cooking time: about 2½ hours

fish stock

1 Put all the ingredients in a large pot and bring to just below boiling point over a low heat. Simmer for 20 minutes, skimming off any scum that rises to the surface.

2 Strain the stock through a cheesecloth-lined strainer. Store in the refrigerator.

3 lb. fish heads and trimmings

1 onion, sliced

1 carrot, sliced

1 small leek, white part only

1 celery stalk, roughly chopped

1 bay leaf

1 thyme sprig

6 parsley sprigs

10 black peppercorns

2 cups dry white wine

2 quarts cold water

Makes 2 quarts
Preparation time: 10 minutes
Cooking time: 20 minutes

All white fish are suitable for making stock, but avoid using oily fish, such as mackerel or herring. You can also use shrimp heads and shells.

vegetable stock

1 Put all the ingredients in a large pot and bring to a boil over a moderate heat. Lower the heat and simmer for 30 minutes, skimming off any scum that rises to the surface.

2 Strain the stock through a cheesecloth-lined strainer. Store in the refrigerator.

1 lb. mixed vegetables, such as equal quantities of carrots, leeks, celery, onion, and mushrooms, chopped

1 garlic clove

6 black peppercorns

1 bouquet garni (2 parsley sprigs, 2 thyme sprigs, and 1 bay leaf)

5 cups cold water

Makes about 1 quart
Preparation time: 5–10 minutes
Cooking time: 45 minutes

"Only the pure of heart can make a good soup."

Ludwig van Beethoven

Garnishes

There are many simple ways to make your soups look as wonderful as they taste. Add a swirl of sour cream or plain yogurt just before serving. Drawing a toothpick gently through the swirl creates a delicate feathered effect. Sprinkle the soup with snipped chives or tiny herb sprigs, such as dill or flat-leaf parsley. Croûtons and crispy fried diced bacon add a delicious contrast in texture to creamy soups.

To make croûtons, remove the crusts from 2 slices of day-old white bread and cut the bread into small squares. Fry over a moderate heat in 2 tablespoons vegetable oil or ½ stick (¼ cup) butter, stirring and tossing constantly. Vary the flavor by adding garlic, anchovies, bacon, or cheese.

Tomatoes

When using tomatoes to make soup it is best to peel them first. To do this, cut a small cross in the base of each tomato, place in a bowl, and cover with boiling water. Within 10–15 seconds, the skins will begin to roll back. Remove the tomatoes and rinse them in cold water, then peel off the skins.

hearty soups

12

arugula & white bean twin soup with basil & walnut pesto

1 To make the white bean soup, drain and rinse the navy or cannellini beans and place in a pot with the water. Bring to a boil, reduce the heat and simmer for 45–60 minutes, or until tender. Transfer the beans, together with the cooking liquid, to a blender or food processor, in batches if necessary, and blend to a purée. Strain through a strainer, pressing with the back of a ladle to extract as much soup as possible. Return the soup to the pot, and season to taste with salt and pepper.

2 To make the pesto, place the basil, parsley, walnuts, and garlic in a blender or food processor, and blend until finely chopped. With the motor running, gradually add the oil in a thin stream until fully incorporated. Scrape the pesto into a bowl, stir in the Parmesan, and season to taste with salt and pepper.

3 To make the arugula soup, melt the butter in a large pot. Add the onion and cook over low heat, stirring occasionally, for 5–6 minutes, until softened, but not colored. Add the potatoes, stir, cover, and cook for 5 minutes. Add the arugula, cover, and cook for 3–4 minutes, stirring occasionally, until just wilted. Add the stock and milk, season to taste with salt and pepper, and simmer for 10 minutes, until the potatoes are tender. Blend the soup in a blender or food processor, in batches if necessary. Strain through a strainer into a clean pot.

4 Reheat the soups separately. Add the cream to the arugula soup, heat gently without boiling, and adjust the seasoning to taste. Adjust the consistency of the white bean soup, by adding more water or stock if needed, so that it is the same consistency as the arugula soup. Using 2 ladles, simultaneously pour the soups into warmed individual soup bowls. Serve drizzled with the basil and walnut pesto.

White Bean Soup:

1 cup dried navy or cannellini beans, soaked overnight

1 quart cold water

salt and pepper

Basil & Walnut Pesto:

½ cup basil leaves

¼ cup flat-leaf parsley

¼ cup walnuts

2 garlic cloves, chopped

½ cup extra-virgin olive oil

½ cup finely grated Parmesan cheese

Arugula Soup:

2 tablespoons butter

1 onion, chopped

2 potatoes, about 8 oz., cut into ¾-inch dice

3½ cups arugula, roughly chopped

1¼ cups Chicken or Vegetable Stock (see pages 7 and 8)

1¼ cups milk

¼ cup heavy cream

Serves 4

Preparation time: 45 minutes plus overnight soaking

Cooking time: 45–60 minutes

mulligatawny soup

1 Heat the oil in a heavy pot. Add the onions and fry, stirring occasionally, until browned. Stir in the curry powder and cook, stirring occasionally, for 2 minutes. Add the garlic, lentils, red pepper, chiles, stock, raisins, and tomatoes, and season with salt and pepper to taste. Bring to a boil, lower the heat, cover, and simmer for 1½ hours.

2 Remove the pot from the heat and set aside to cool slightly. Strain the soup or blend in a blender or food processor until smooth. Return to the pot and heat through.

3 Ladle the soup into warmed soup bowls, garnish with saffron rice, if you like, and serve immediately.

2 tablespoons vegetable oil

2 large onions, chopped

1 tablespoon curry powder

2 garlic cloves, crushed

1 cup green lentils, washed and drained

1 red pepper, cored, seeded, and chopped

3 dried chiles, chopped

5 cups Chicken Stock (see page 7)

3 tablespoons seedless raisins

¾ cup peeled (see page 9), seeded, and chopped tomatoes

1 tablespoon tomato paste

salt and pepper

saffron rice (see below), to garnish (optional)

Serves 8
Preparation time: 10 minutes
Cooking time: 1¾ hours

■ To make saffron rice, cook 2-3 tablespoons of long-grain rice in boiling salted water, with a few strands of saffron, for 15 minutes, until tender.

armenian onion & lentil soup

2 tablespoons pearl barley

⅔ cup water

2 quarts Beef Stock (see page 7)

2½ cups thinly sliced onions

⅔ cup green lentils, washed and drained

1 teaspoon dried tarragon

2 teaspoons paprika

pinch of cayenne pepper

¼ teaspoon sugar

3 tablespoons dry white wine

salt and pepper

To Garnish:

2 tablespoons butter

3 tablespoons finely chopped mild onion

Serves 8
Preparation time: 15 minutes
Cooking time: about 1¾ hours

1 Put the barley into a pot with the water. Bring the mixture to a boil. Lower the heat, partially cover, and simmer, stirring occasionally, for 25–30 minutes, or until all the water is absorbed.

2 Add the stock, onions, lentils, tarragon, paprika, cayenne, sugar, and wine. Bring the mixture to a boil, lower the heat, partially cover, and simmer for about 1¼ hours. Add more water if the soup is too thick. Season to taste with salt and pepper.

3 For the garnish, melt the butter in a small frying pan over medium heat. Add the onion and cook, stirring occasionally, for 5 minutes, or until soft and golden.

4 Carefully ladle the soup into warmed bowls, garnish with the fried onion, and serve immediately.

quick chestnut & bacon soup

1 Melt the butter in a large, heavy pot over medium heat. Add the bacon and cook, stirring occasionally, for 2–3 minutes, until lightly browned. Reduce the heat and add the shallots or onion, fennel, and celery, and cook for 6–8 minutes, or until softened.

2 Add the chestnuts to the pan, together with the stock and milk, and season to taste with salt and pepper. Bring to a boil, reduce the heat and simmer for 15–20 minutes, or until the chestnuts are tender.

3 Meanwhile, prepare the croûtons. Rub the ciabatta slices with the garlic halves. Pour the olive oil into a small plate, dip the bread in the oil and place under a hot broiler until toasted to light golden.

4 Blend the soup in a blender or food processor, in batches if necessary. Strain through a strainer, return to the pot and bring back to a boil. Ladle into warm serving bowls, add a swirl of cream to each, and serve with the garlic croûtons.

■ Ciabatta is a rustic Italian bread made with olive oil and often flavored with herbs, olives, or sun-dried tomatoes. The texture is light and the crust is crisp.

½ stick (¼ cup) butter

6–7 slices bacon, chopped

3 shallots or 1 large onion, chopped

½ small fennel bulb, chopped

1 celery stalk, chopped

8 oz. vacuum-packed cooked chestnuts

2½ cups Chicken or Vegetable Stock (see pages 7 and 8)

2½ cups milk

salt and pepper

heavy cream, to serve

Croûtons:

8 slices ciabatta

2 garlic cloves, cut in half

⅓ cup extra-virgin olive oil

Serves 4

Preparation time: 15 minutes

Cooking time: 25–35 minutes

coconut & plantain soup

1 Heat the oil in a large pot. Add the onion, garlic, chile, ginger, and lime zest, and cook, stirring occasionally, for 8–10 minutes, or until softened. Add the tomatoes and cook for a further 5 minutes.

2 To peel the plantains, cut off one end and, using a small sharp knife, slit the skin down its length, then peel it off sideways. Chop the flesh and add to the pan, together with the allspice, thyme, stock and coconut milk. Season to taste with salt and pepper, bring to a boil, reduce the heat and simmer for 30 minutes or until the plantains are tender.

3 Meanwhile, place the Brazil or macadamia nuts on a baking sheet and place in a preheated oven, 325°F, for 10–15 minutes, or until light golden. Remove from the oven, set aside to cool, then chop finely.

4 Remove the soup from the heat and discard the thyme sprig. Blend the soup in a blender or food processor, in batches if necessary. Strain through a strainer and return to the pot to reheat. Add the lime juice and adjust the seasoning to taste. Serve in warmed bowls, sprinkled with the chopped Brazil or macadamia nuts.

2 tablespoons vegetable oil

1 onion, finely chopped

1–2 garlic cloves, crushed

1 fresh red chile, seeded and finely chopped

1-inch piece of fresh ginger root, grated

finely grated zest and juice of 1 lime

2 tomatoes, about 10 oz., skinned (see page 9) and chopped

2 large semi-ripe plantains or green bananas

6 allspice berries, crushed

1 thyme sprig

5 cups Chicken Stock (see page 7)

a 14 fl oz. can unsweetened coconut milk

salt and pepper

⅔ cup shelled Brazil or macadamia nuts, to serve

Serves 6

Preparation time: 20 minutes

Cooking time: 45 minutes

bean soup

½ cup navy beans, soaked overnight in cold water to cover

¼ cup red kidney beans, soaked overnight in cold water to cover

2 tablespoons butter

2 large onions, chopped

2 garlic cloves, crushed

2 celery stalks, chopped

2 large carrots, chopped

½ cup fresh peas or frozen peas, defrosted

a 14-oz. can tomatoes

½ cup dry red wine

1¼ cups Chicken Stock (see page 7)

1 bouquet garni

¾–1 cup sliced zucchini

1 tablespoon Worcestershire sauce

1 tablespoon tomato paste

salt and pepper

Pistou:

4 garlic cloves

1 bunch fresh basil

¼ cup olive oil

¼ cup pine nuts

1 Drain the navy and kidney beans, rinse in cold water, and drain again. Put them into a large pot, cover with cold water, and bring to a boil. Boil vigorously for 10 minutes, then lower the heat, cover, and simmer for 1¼ hours, or until the beans are tender. Drain and set aside.

2 Melt the butter in a large, heavy pot. Add the onions and fry over a medium heat for 5–6 minutes, or until golden. Add the garlic, celery, carrots, peas, tomatoes, together with their juice, wine, stock, and bouquet garni, and season with salt and pepper to taste. Bring to a boil, lower the heat, cover, and simmer for 20 minutes.

3 Stir in the zucchini, Worcestershire sauce, and tomato paste. Continue cooking for 5 minutes, then add the cooked beans and heat through.

4 Meanwhile, make the pistou. Pound the garlic, basil, oil, and nuts to a smooth paste using a mortar and a pestle. Mix the pistou into the soup just before serving.

Serves 6–8

Preparation time: 20 minutes plus soaking

Cooking time: 2½ hours

pumpkin, garlic & peanut butter soup

6–8 garlic cloves, unpeeled

3 tablespoons olive oil

1 large onion, chopped

2 celery stalks, chopped

1 leek, chopped

6 allspice berries, crushed

1 thyme sprig

1 bay leaf

2 tomatoes, peeled (see page 9) and chopped

¼ cup peanut butter

1½ lb. peeled pumpkin, cubed

1½ quarts Chicken Stock (see page 7)

salt and pepper

a scant cup sour cream, to serve

Chile Breadsticks:

2 cups all purpose flour

½ teaspoon salt

4½ teaspoons fast-action dry yeast

1 tablespoon olive oil

1 fresh red or green chile, seeded and very finely chopped

¾ cup warm water

Serves 4–6
Preparation time: 45 minutes
Cooking time: 1 hour 40 minutes

1 To make the breadsticks, sift the flour and salt into the bowl of a food processor, add the yeast, oil, and chile. With the machine running, gradually add enough water to form a soft dough. Turn the dough onto a lightly floured surface and knead for 5 minutes, or until smooth and elastic. Divide the dough into 16 pieces and roll each into a stick about 11 inches long and ½ inch thick. Place on a lightly oiled baking sheet and let rise for 15–20 minutes. Bake in a preheated oven, 300°F, for 1 hour, or until lightly browned and crisp.

2 Increase the oven temperature to 350°F. Place the garlic cloves in a baking pan and toss with 1 tablespoon of the oil. Cook for 15–20 minutes, or until softened. Leave to cool, then pop the soft flesh out of the skins and reserve.

3 Heat the remaining oil in a large, heavy pot. Add the onion, celery, and leek, and cook over low heat, stirring frequently, for 8–10 minutes, or until softened. Add all the remaining ingredients, including the baked garlic cloves, bring to a boil, and simmer for 20–30 minutes, or until the vegetables are soft. Remove and discard the bay leaf and thyme.

4 Blend the soup in a blender or food processor. Strain through a strainer, return to the pot, and bring back to a boil. Top each bowl of soup with a spoonful of sour cream, and serve accompanied by the chile breadsticks.

spanish chickpea soup

1 Drain the chickpeas, rinse under cold water, and drain again. Put the ham hock in a deep pot and cover with cold water. Bring the water to a boil, then drain the ham, discarding the water.

2 Return the ham hock to the clean pot. Add the chickpeas, onion, garlic, bay leaf, thyme, marjoram, parsley, and the water. Bring the mixture to a boil, then lower the heat, partially cover, and simmer for 1½ hours. Remove and discard the onion, bay leaf, and herb sprigs. Lift out the ham, cut it into small pieces, and set aside.

3 Add the stock, potatoes, and cabbage to the pot and simmer for a further 30 minutes. Add the reserved ham pieces to the soup and cook for a further 10 minutes. Season with salt and pepper to taste. Serve in warmed soup bowls.

1 cup dried chickpeas, covered with boiling water and soaked overnight

1 small boneless smoked ham hock, about 1–1½ lb.

1 onion, studded with 4 cloves

2 garlic cloves, crushed

1 bay leaf

1 thyme sprig

1 marjoram sprig

1 parsley sprig

2 quarts water

2 quarts Chicken Stock (see page 7)

10–12 oz. (around 3 small-to-medium) potatoes, cut into ½-inch cubes

4½–5 cups shredded Savoy cabbage

salt and pepper

Serves 8–10

Preparation time: 15 minutes plus soaking

Cooking time: 2½–2¾ hours

risi e bisi with prosciutto

1½ lb. fresh young peas in the pod

3 tablespoons olive oil

1 onion, chopped

5 cups Chicken Stock (see page 7)

1 cup risotto (Arborio) rice

large pinch of sugar

2 tablespoons chopped flat-leaf parsley

1 cup finely grated Parmesan cheese plus extra to serve

salt and pepper

To Garnish:

4 slices prosciutto

1 tablespoon olive oil

Serves 4
Preparation time: 10 minutes
Cooking time: 25–40 minutes

1 Shell the peas. Heat the oil in a large, heavy pot over medium heat. Add the onion and cook, stirring, for 5–10 minutes, until softened but not colored.

2 Add the stock, bring to a boil, reduce the heat, and add the peas. Simmer gently for 5 minutes, then stir in the rice. Season with salt, pepper, and a pinch of sugar. Cover and simmer gently, stirring occasionally, for 15–20 minutes, until the rice is tender.

3 For the garnish, cut each slice of prosciutto in half lengthwise. Heat the oil in a large frying pan, add the prosciutto strips, and fry over a high heat for 10–15 seconds, until crisp. Drain on paper towels.

4 Stir the parsley and Parmesan into the hot soup. Serve the soup in individual bowls, each topped with 2 pieces of the prosciutto. Serve a small bowl of extra grated Parmesan separately.

pronto provençal soup

¼ cup extra-virgin olive oil

1 large onion, chopped

1 garlic clove, crushed

1 small red pepper, cored, seeded, and cut into ½-inch cubes

1 small yellow pepper, cored, seeded, and cut into ½-inch cubes

1 eggplant, about 10 oz., cut into ½-inch cubes

2 zucchini, about 8 oz., cut into ½-inch cubes

4 tomatoes, about 10 oz., skinned (see page 9) and chopped

1 tablespoon wine vinegar

2 cups Chicken or Vegetable Stock (see pages 7 and 8)

1 thyme sprig

½ teaspoon coriander seeds, crushed

a generous ⅓ cup chopped pitted black olives

2 tablespoons chopped parsley

1 tablespoon chopped basil

salt and pepper

To Garnish:

4 large plum tomatoes

1 small garlic clove, crushed

1 tablespoon olive oil

¼ teaspoon salt

½ cup Swiss or fontina cheese, finely grated

1 tablespoon chopped parsley

cayenne pepper

1 First prepare the garnish. Cut the tomatoes in half lengthwise and, holding them over a bowl, scoop out the seeds with a spoon; reserve the seeds. Place the tomato halves on a lightly oiled baking sheet with sides. Mix together the garlic, oil, and salt, and drizzle over the tomatoes. Place in a preheated oven, 300°F, for 30 minutes.

2 Meanwhile, heat the oil in a large pot over low heat. Add the onion and garlic and cook, stirring occasionally, for 5–10 minutes, or until softened, but not colored. Add the peppers, eggplant, and zucchini, and cook for a further 10 minutes. Add the tomatoes with the reserved seeds and juice from the plum tomatoes, the vinegar, stock, thyme, and coriander seeds. Bring to a boil, reduce the heat, and simmer for 15–20 minutes. Add the olives after 10–15 minutes. Season with salt and pepper to taste.

3 To finish the garnish, mix the cheese with the chopped parsley and a pinch of cayenne pepper. Remove the tomatoes from the oven and place a spoonful of the cheese mixture into each. Return to the oven for 5–10 minutes, or until the cheese is melted and bubbling.

4 Reheat the soup, if necessary, and stir in the parsley and basil. Pour into individual bowls and top each with 2 baked tomato halves.

Serves 4

Preparation time: 25 minutes

Cooking time: 30–40 minutes

green cabbage soup with meatballs

1 Melt the butter in a large, heavy pot. Add the cabbage and sugar and cook, stirring constantly, until the cabbage is golden. Add the stock, allspice, and peppercorns. Lower the heat, cover, and simmer for 30–35 minutes, or until the cabbage is tender. Season with salt to taste.

2 To make the meatballs, place the breadcrumbs in a bowl, add the water and set aside to soak for 3 minutes. Then add the veal, pork, egg yolks, salt, pepper, Worcestershire sauce, and Dijon mustard. Stir the mixture vigorously with a fork until it is very smooth. Shape the mixture into balls, the size of walnuts, between the palms of your hands.

3 Bring the soup to a boil and add the meatballs one at a time. Lower the heat and simmer gently, uncovered, for 10 minutes. Transfer the soup to a warmed tureen and serve immediately.

½ stick (¼ cup) butter

1 green cabbage, about 1¾ lb., coarsely shredded

2 teaspoons sugar

1½ quarts Beef Stock (see page 7)

3 allspice berries

6 white peppercorns

salt

Meatballs:

2 tablespoons dry white breadcrumbs

⅔ cup water

½ lb. lean ground veal

½ lb. lean ground pork

2 egg yolks

1 teaspoon salt

¼ teaspoon freshly ground white pepper

1 teaspoon Worcestershire sauce

1 teaspoon Dijon mustard

Serves 4–6

Preparation time: 25 minutes

Cooking time: 45–50 minutes

goulash soup

3 tablespoons vegetable oil

1½ lb. boneless lean beef stewing meat, cut into 1-inch cubes

2 onions, chopped

2 garlic cloves, crushed

2 celery stalks, chopped

3 tablespoons paprika

1 tablespoon caraway seeds

5 cups Beef Stock (see page 7)

2½ cups water

¼ teaspoon dried thyme

2 bay leaves

¼ teaspoon Tabasco sauce

3 tablespoons tomato paste

½ lb. (2 small-to-medium) potatoes, cut into ½-inch dice

3 carrots, cut into ½-inch dice

6–8 teaspoons sour cream, to garnish (optional)

Serves 6–8
Preparation time: 10–15 minutes
Cooking time: 1¼ hours

1 Heat the oil in a heavy pot. Add the beef, in batches, and brown over medium heat. As each batch browns, transfer it to paper towels to drain. Then cook the onions, garlic, and celery in the oil until transparent.

2 Remove the pot from the heat and stir in the paprika, caraway seeds, stock, and water. Add the thyme, bay leaves, Tabasco sauce, and tomato paste, stir well, then add the cooked beef. Bring the mixture to a boil, then lower the heat, partially cover, and simmer for 30 minutes.

3 Add the diced potatoes and carrots and simmer for a further 30 minutes, or until the potatoes are tender. Remove and discard the bay leaves. Serve the soup immediately in warmed bowls, garnishing each portion with a teaspoon of sour cream, if you like.

potato & bacon soup

1 Coarsely chop the bacon. Heat the oil in a heavy pot, add the chopped bacon, onion, and garlic to the pot and cook over medium heat, stirring frequently, for 8–10 minutes, or until the onion is light brown and the bacon is fairly crisp. Add the stock, water, potatoes, leeks, cabbage, marjoram, nutmeg, and Worcestershire sauce, and season with pepper to taste. Bring the mixture to a boil. Lower the heat, cover, and simmer, stirring occasionally, for 25 minutes.

2 Blend 2½ cups of the soup mixture in a blender or food processor for about 2 seconds, then return to the pot. Stir well and cook the soup for a further 10 minutes over a low heat. Season with salt to taste. Just before serving, stir in the parsley, if using. Serve in individual warmed soup bowls.

6 oz. bacon

1 tablespoon olive oil

1 onion, finely chopped

2 garlic cloves, finely chopped

2½ cups Chicken Stock (see page 7)

5 cups water

1½ lb. potatoes, diced

3 leeks, sliced

10 oz. (4½–5 cups) shredded cabbage

1 teaspoon chopped marjoram

¼ teaspoon grated nutmeg

1 teaspoon Worcestershire sauce

3–4 tablespoons finely chopped parsley (optional)

salt and pepper

Serves 8

Preparation time: 20 minutes

Cooking time: 1 hour

bean thread noodle soup

2 tablespoons vegetable oil

½ lb. ground pork

1 quart Chicken Stock (see page 7)

4 oz. bean thread noodles

4 scallions, cut into 1-inch lengths

½ onion, finely chopped

2 tablespoons fish sauce

2 tablespoons salt

½ lb. raw shrimp, peeled and deveined

2 celery stalks with leaves, chopped

pepper

Garlic Mixture:

1 garlic clove, crushed

1 teaspoon chopped cilantro stem

¼ teaspoon pepper

Serves 4–6
Preparation time: 10 minutes
Cooking time: 10 minutes

1 To make the garlic mixture, pound the garlic, cilantro, and pepper using a mortar and pestle. Heat the oil in a wok or deep frying pan, add the garlic mixture and stir-fry for 1 minute.

2 Add the ground pork and stir-fry for 3 minutes, then pour in the stock and bring to a boil. Stir in the noodles, scallions, onion, fish sauce, and salt. Bring the soup back to a boil and cook for 3 minutes. Lower the heat, add the shrimp and celery, and simmer for a further 2 minutes.

3 Transfer to a warmed serving bowl, season with pepper, and serve immediately.

cream of chicken soup

1 large onion, chopped
2 celery stalks, chopped
2 large carrots, chopped
1 leek, chopped
one 2½ lb. chicken
1 bouquet garni
grated zest and juice of ½ lemon
salt
3 tablespoons butter
3 tablespoons all-purpose flour
2 egg yolks (optional)
2⅔ cups heavy cream

Serves 6
Preparation time: 15 minutes plus cooling
Cooking time: 1¼ hours

1 Put all the vegetables and chicken in a large pot and pour over enough water to cover. Add the bouquet garni, lemon zest and juice, and season with salt to taste. Bring to a boil over a low heat, skim, then cover and simmer for 1 hour, or until the chicken is tender.

2 Take out the chicken and cut off about 8 oz. meat. Dice and set aside. Strain the stock and reserve 5 cups. Leave to cool, then skim off any fat.

3 Melt the butter in a pot, stir in the flour, and cook, stirring constantly, for 1 minute, without browning. Gradually stir in the reserved stock. Bring to a boil, stirring constantly. Simmer for 2 minutes, then add the diced chicken and heat through.

4 Blend the egg yolks, if using, and cream together. Remove the soup from the heat and stir in the cream mixture. Serve immediately.

■ The rest of the cooked chicken may be used for another dish, such as a pie, or as a pizza topping.

speedy watercress soup with poached quail eggs

½ stick (¼ cup) butter

1 onion, finely chopped

½ lb. (2 small-to-medium) potatoes, cut into ½-inch cubes

10 oz. watercress, roughly chopped

1 quart Chicken or Vegetable Stock (see pages 7 and 8)

1¼ cups light cream

12 quail eggs or 4 small chicken eggs

salt and pepper

1 cup finely grated Parmesan cheese, for sprinkling

Serves 4
Preparation time: 5 minutes plus cooling
Cooking time: 20–25 minutes

1 Melt the butter in a large, heavy pot. Add the onion and cook over low heat, stirring occasionally, for 8–10 minutes, or until softened, but not colored. Stir in the potatoes and watercress, cover, and cook, stirring occasionally, for 3–5 minutes, or until the watercress has just wilted.

2 Add the stock and season to taste with salt and pepper. Bring the soup to a boil, lower the heat, and simmer for 6–8 minutes, until the potatoes are tender.

3 Purée the soup in a blender or food processor, in batches if necessary, until smooth. Strain through a strainer and return to the pot. Add the cream, adjust the seasoning to taste, and gently heat the soup without boiling.

4 Poach the quail or chicken eggs in a pan of gently simmering water, until cooked to taste. Remove the eggs with a slotted spoon and drain well on paper towels. Place 3 quail eggs in each serving bowl or one if using chicken eggs. Ladle the soup over the eggs and serve sprinkled with the grated Parmesan.

■ Quail eggs are available from gourmet grocery stores. If you cannot find them, chicken eggs can be substituted.

fish & seafood soups

quick shrimp & okra soup

1 Melt the butter in a pot. Add the onion and celery, cover, and cook over medium heat until the onion softens, but has not browned. Add the stock and rice to the pot. Heat until just below boiling point, cover, and cook gently for 20 minutes, or until the rice is tender.

2 Prepare the okra by cutting away the conical cap from the stalk end, then cut the pods into ½-inch slices.

3 Uncover the pot and add the tomatoes, okra, shrimp, and ham, and cook, stirring frequently, for a further 5–8 minutes. Serve the soup in warmed bowls, garnished with small parsley leaves.

½ stick (¼ cup) butter

1 onion, finely chopped

2 cups finely chopped celery stalks

1 quart Fish Stock (see page 8)

¼ cup long-grain white rice

1 generous cup okra

2 tomatoes, peeled (see page 9) and finely chopped

1¾ cups cooked peeled shrimp, defrosted if frozen

2–3 slices cooked ham, cut into fine strips (around ½ cup)

small parsley leaves, to garnish

Serves 4–6

Preparation time: 15 minutes

Cooking time: 30–35 minutes

Okra, also known as bhindi and gumbo, are small, bright green, five-sided, edible seed pods. They are featured in Indian and Caribbean cooking and are widely used in Louisiana and other southern states for the silky smooth finish they give to soups and stews.

lobster bisque

¾ stick (⅓ cup) butter

2 medium carrots, roughly chopped

1 celery stalk, chopped

1 onion, roughly chopped

1 lobster or crawfish shell, legs, and any scraps of leftover flesh (from seafood prepared for another recipe)

6 black peppercorns

pinch of salt

1 small bunch of parsley

½ cup all-purpose flour

2 teaspoons coarsely chopped mint

⅔ cup heavy cream

warm French bread, to serve (optional)

Serves 4

Preparation time: 15 minutes plus chilling

Cooking time: 40–45 minutes

1 Melt 2 tablespoons of the butter in a large, heavy pot. Add the carrots, celery, and onion, cover, and sweat over low heat for 5–7 minutes. Break up the shells and legs of the lobster or crawfish, and pack on top of the vegetables. Just cover the seafood with cold water and add the peppercorns, salt, and parsley. Simmer over a low heat for 30–45 minutes. Strain through a strainer into a bowl and reserve.

2 Melt the remaining butter in the clean pot. Stir in the flour and cook, stirring constantly, for 2–3 minutes. Remove from the heat and gradually stir in the reserved stock. Return the pot to the heat and bring to a boil, stirring constantly. Taste, and adjust the seasoning if necessary. Simmer for 5–6 minutes.

3 Add the chopped mint and stir in the heavy cream. Also add any reserved flakes of shellfish flesh. Heat through gently and serve with warmed French bread, if you like.

quick & easy shrimp bisque

½ stick (¼ cup) butter

1 small carrot, finely chopped

½ small onion, finely chopped

½ celery stalk, finely chopped

1 lb. raw shrimp in their shells

1 cup dry white wine

2 tablespoons brandy

5 cups Fish Stock (see page 8)

1 bouquet garni

2 tablespoons long-grain rice

½ cup heavy cream

pinch of cayenne pepper

salt and pepper

To Garnish:

¼ cup chopped parsley

1 small mango, peeled and finely chopped

Serves 4
Preparation time: 20 minutes
Cooking time: 30–40 minutes

1 Melt the butter in a large, heavy pot. Add the carrot, onion, and celery, and cook, stirring occasionally, for 8–10 minutes, or until softened and light golden. Increase the heat, add the shrimp, and cook for about 3–4 minutes, or until the shells turn pink all over.

2 Add the wine and brandy, bring to a boil, then lower the heat and simmer for 3–4 minutes, until the shrimp are cooked. Remove the shrimp and leave to cool slightly. When cool enough to handle, peel them, reserving their shells. Remove the black veins running down the back, chop the flesh, and set aside.

3 Bring the liquid back to a boil and boil rapidly for 2–3 minutes, or until reduced by one-third. Add the reserved shrimp shells, together with the fish stock, bouquet garni, and rice. Bring to a boil, reduce the heat, and simmer gently for 15–20 minutes, or until the rice is tender.

4 Remove and discard the bouquet garni. Purée the soup, including the shrimp shells, in a blender or food processor, with three-quarters of the shrimp meat. Strain through a fine strainer into a clean pot, pressing with the back of a ladle to push through as much liquid as possible. Add the cream, and season to taste with salt, pepper, and cayenne pepper. Add the reserved chopped shrimp, and heat gently for 1–2 minutes until hot, but not boiling. Serve sprinkled with chopped parsley and mango.

The herbs used to make a bouquet garni may vary. A fairly standard combination is a bay leaf and 1 sprig each of marjoram, thyme, and parsley tied together.

la bourride

2 leeks, thinly sliced

1 onion, thinly sliced

3 garlic cloves

1 lb. potatoes, thinly sliced

3 lb. firm white fish, filleted and cut into bite-size pieces

2 quarts Fish Stock (see page 8)

olive oil, for frying

1 loaf French bread, thickly sliced

Aïoli:

3 garlic cloves, finely chopped

2 egg yolks

1 cup extra-virgin olive oil

lemon juice

salt and pepper

Serves 8
Preparation time: 30 minutes
Cooking time: 20–25 minutes

1 First, make the aïoli. Crush the garlic and a pinch of salt, using the back of a spoon. Beat in the egg yolks with an electric mixer until thick and creamy. Beat in the olive oil, a few drops at a time. When the mixture begins to thicken, add the oil in a thin stream, beating vigorously. Stir in the lemon juice, salt, and pepper to taste. Cover and chill until required.

2 Put the leeks, onion, 2 of the garlic cloves, and the potatoes in a large pot and place the fish on top. Cover with the stock and poach for about 10 minutes, or until the potatoes are tender and the fish is just cooked. Different varieties and thicknesses of fish cook at different speeds so be careful not to let it overcook. With a slotted spoon, transfer the cooked fish, leeks, and potatoes to a heated dish and keep warm.

3 Bring the remaining stock to a boil and continue boiling until it has reduced to one-third of the quantity. Remove from the heat and set aside to cool slightly. Gradually strain the stock into the aïoli, beating constantly. Then gently heat the soup in a pot, but do not let it boil.

4 Rub the inside of a frying pan with the remaining garlic clove and heat the olive oil. Fry the slices of bread in the oil until lightly browned on both sides, and put a slice in the base of each soup bowl. Place the fish, leeks, and potatoes on top, ladle the soup over, and serve immediately.

smoked haddock chowder

1 lb. potatoes, cut into ½-inch cubes

1 onion, finely chopped

1 bay leaf

½ teaspoon chopped marjoram

2½ cups water

1 lb. skinned smoked haddock fillet, coarsely chopped

¼ teaspoon grated nutmeg

2 cups milk

freshly ground white pepper

To Garnish:

2 tablespoons finely chopped marjoram

croûtons (optional, see page 9)

Serves 4–6
Preparation time: 10–15 minutes
Cooking time: 35 minutes

1 Combine the potatoes, onion, bay leaf, marjoram, and water in a pot. Bring the mixture to a boil, then lower the heat, cover, and simmer for 5 minutes.

2 Add the haddock fillet, nutmeg, and milk, and season with white pepper to taste. Partially cover, and simmer for 20 minutes. Remove and discard the bay leaf.

3 Serve the chowder in warmed soup bowls, garnished with finely chopped marjoram and croûtons, if using.

smoked haddock & corn soup with wild rice & bacon croûtons

⅓ cup wild rice

½ lb. smoked haddock

2½ cups milk

1 bay leaf

½ stick (¼ cup) butter

1 large onion, chopped

1 leek, sliced

1 celery stalk, chopped

1 garlic clove, crushed

1 tablespoon thyme leaves

1 quart Chicken Stock (see page 7)

pinch of grated nutmeg

⅔ cup corn, defrosted if frozen

salt and pepper

2 tablespoons chopped parsley, to garnish

Bacon Croûtons:

3 tablespoons olive oil

10 slices bacon, cut into strips

2 slices bread, crusts removed, cut into ½-inch cubes

Serves 4
Preparation time: 15 minutes
Cooking time: 1 hour 20 minutes

1 Place the rice in a small saucepan and cover with cold water. Bring to a boil, reduce the heat, and simmer for 40–45 minutes, until tender. Drain and set aside.

2 Place the haddock, milk, and bay leaf in a saucepan, bring to a boil, reduce the heat, and simmer for 8–10 minutes, until just cooked. Remove the fish with a slotted spoon and set aside to cool. Remove the skin and any remaining bones, and flake the flesh with a fork. Strain and reserve the milk.

3 Melt the butter in a heavy pot. Add the onion, leek, celery, and garlic, and cook over a low heat, stirring occasionally, for 8–10 minutes, until softened, but not colored. Add the thyme, stock, and reserved milk. Season to taste with salt, pepper, and nutmeg. Bring to a boil, reduce the heat, and simmer for 10 minutes. Add the corn and cook for 5 minutes, then add the rice and flaked haddock, and heat for a few minutes. Adjust the seasoning to taste.

4 To make the bacon croûtons, heat the oil in a large frying pan. Add the bacon and fry for 5–6 minutes or until crisp. Remove with a slotted spoon, drain on paper towels, and reserve. Add the bread cubes to the pan and cook, turning frequently, for 4–5 minutes, or until crisp and golden brown. Drain on paper towels, then toss with the reserved bacon. Serve the soup sprinkled with the bacon croûtons and chopped parsley.

speedy genoese fish soup

1 Melt the butter in a large pot. Add the onion and fry over low heat, stirring occasionally, for 2–3 minutes, until softened, but not colored. Add the celery and bacon to the pot, and continue cooking over low heat for a few more minutes.

2 Add the tomatoes, wine, stock, and marjoram, and season to taste with salt and pepper. Simmer for 10 minutes.

3 Add the fish and cook for 5 minutes. Finally, add the shrimp and simmer for a further 2–3 minutes. Taste, and adjust the seasoning, if necessary, and serve hot, garnished with chopped parsley. Offer warm rolls with the soup, if you like.

2 tablespoons butter

1 onion, chopped

3 celery stalks, chopped

4–5 slices bacon, chopped

a 14-oz. can chopped tomatoes

⅔ cup dry white wine

1¼ cups Fish Stock (see page 8)

½ teaspoon chopped marjoram

1 lb. monkfish or cod, boned, skinned, and diced

a scant cup cooked peeled shrimp

salt and pepper

2 tablespoons chopped parsley, to garnish

warm rolls, to serve (optional)

Serves 4–6
Preparation time: 20 minutes
Cooking time: 25–30 minutes

Garlic lovers can add a clove of garlic to this tasty soup to give extra flavor. Add the crushed or finely chopped garlic to the pot with melted butter, along with the chopped onion, then continue as above.

1 Cut the mackerel, whiting, and haddock or cod into chunks. Heat the oil in a large, heavy pot. Add the garlic and onions, and fry over low heat, stirring occasionally, for 3–5 minutes, or until the onions are transparent, but not brown. Add the fish chunks and cook, uncovered, over medium heat, stirring occasionally, for 10 minutes.

2 Add the shrimp and tomatoes. Dissolve the saffron strands in the hot fish stock and add to the pot, together with the bay leaf and parsley. Season with salt and pepper to taste. Stir and bring to a boil. Lower the heat, cover, and simmer for 15 minutes, then add the mussels and continue cooking for a further 10 minutes, or until the fish is tender and flakes easily when tested with the tip of a knife.

3 Discard the bay leaf, parsley sprigs, and any mussels that have not opened. Place the bread in a warmed soup tureen, and ladle the soup over it. Sprinkle with the chopped parsley before serving, if you like.

bouillabaisse

1 lb. mackerel fillets

1 lb. whiting fillets

1 lb. haddock or cod fillets

¼ cup olive oil

2 garlic cloves, finely chopped

2 onions, chopped

¾ cup raw peeled shrimp

6 tomatoes, peeled (see page 9) and chopped

½ teaspoon saffron strands

1½ quarts hot Fish Stock (see page 8)

1 bay leaf

3 parsley sprigs

10–12 live mussels, scrubbed and debearded

6–8 slices French bread

salt and pepper

2 tablespoons finely chopped parsley, to garnish (optional)

Serves 6–8

Preparation time: 30–40 minutes

Cooking time: 30–35 minutes

classic clam chowder

48–60 littleneck or cherrystone clams (discard any that do not shut immediately when sharply tapped)

3 tablespoons butter

about 10 slices bacon, diced

2 large onions, finely chopped

2 celery stalks, diced

1–2 leeks, sliced

2 tablespoons finely chopped parsley plus extra to garnish

2 bay leaves

leaves from 1 thyme sprig

1 quart water

grated nutmeg

4–5 medium potatoes, diced

2 tablespoons all-purpose flour

1–2 teaspoons Worcestershire sauce

finely ground sea salt (optional) and pepper

Serves 6–8
Preparation time: 25–45 minutes
Cooking time: 35–40 minutes

1 Put the clams on a baking sheet in a preheated oven, 400°F, for 2–3 minutes, or until they open slightly, then remove and pry the shells apart. Open the shells over a bowl to catch all the clam juice. Snip off the inedible black-tipped necks (they look like a little tube), roughly chop the coral-colored and pink flesh, and leave the softer body meat whole.

2 Melt 2 tablespoons of the butter in a large pot. Add the bacon and cook for about 5 minutes, until the fat starts to run. Add the onions, cover, and cook gently for 10 minutes. Add the celery, leeks, parsley, bay leaves, and thyme, and cook for a further 5 minutes. Add the reserved clam juice, the water, nutmeg, and pepper to taste. Stir well, taste, and season with salt, if necessary. Add the potatoes and bring to a boil. Simmer gently for about 10 minutes, until the potatoes are almost tender.

3 Meanwhile, cream the flour with the remaining butter to a smooth paste and set aside. Add the clams to the pot and simmer very gently for 3–4 minutes. Do not boil, or the clams will be tough and rubbery. Add a piece of the butter and flour paste to the pot, stirring well. When it has been fully incorporated, stir in a little more, and continue until all the paste has been added. Stir for another 3–4 minutes or until the soup thickens slightly.

4 Increase the heat briefly for 10 seconds, then remove from the heat. Add the Worcestershire sauce, stir, and serve immediately, garnished with chopped parsley.

mussel chowder

1 Heat the olive oil in a heavy pot. Add the bacon and cook over medium heat, stirring occasionally, until browned. Add the onions, celery, and green pepper, and cook, stirring frequently, for 5 minutes, or until the vegetables soften. Add the stock, potatoes, bay leaf, and marjoram. Bring to a boil, then lower the heat, cover, and simmer for 15–20 minutes, or until the potatoes are tender.

2 In a small bowl, blend the flour with half of the milk. Whisk the mixture into the chowder, bring to a boil, stirring constantly, then gradually add the remaining milk. Season with salt and pepper to taste.

3 Lower the heat, add the mussels, and simmer gently, stirring occasionally, for 5 minutes. Do not boil. Stir in the cream and pour the chowder into a warmed soup tureen. Garnish with chopped parsley, if using, and serve immediately with crusty French bread, if you like.

2 tablespoons olive oil

½ lb. bacon, chopped

2 onions, finely chopped

1 celery stalk, finely chopped

1 green bell pepper, cored, seeded, and finely chopped

2 cups Fish Stock (see page 8)

½ lb. (around 2 small-to-medium) potatoes, diced

1 bay leaf

½ teaspoon chopped marjoram

3 tablespoons all-purpose flour

1¼ cups milk

1 lb. shelled mussels, defrosted if frozen

⅔ cup light cream

salt and pepper

1 tablespoon finely chopped parsley, to garnish (optional)

crusty French bread, to serve (optional)

Serves 4–6

Preparation time: 10–15 minutes

Cooking time: 30 minutes

Fresh mussels are preferable for this chowder but frozen or tinned mussels can be used as a substitute.

mussel soup with saffron, basil & spinach

1 Place the saffron in a small bowl, pour in the boiling water, and set aside to infuse. Discard any mussels that are broken or do not shut immediately when sharply tapped with a knife. Place a large colander over a bowl.

2 Pour the white wine into a large pot. Bring the wine to a boil, add the mussels, cover with a tight-fitting lid, and cook, shaking the pot frequently for 2–3 minutes, or until the mussels have opened. Tip the mussels into the colander, discarding any that have not opened. Strain the mussel liquid through a cheesecloth-lined strainer, and set aside.

3 Heat the oil in a pot over low heat. Add the shallots and garlic, and cook over low heat, stirring occasionally, for 5–6 minutes, until softened, but not colored. Add the reserved mussel liquid, the cream, the saffron and its infused liquid, and heat to just below boiling point. Reduce the heat and add the spinach, half of the basil, and all the mussels. Cook gently for 2 minutes, without boiling, then remove from the heat. Stir in the remaining basil and serve at once.

pinch of saffron threads

½ cup boiling water

1½ lb. live mussels, scrubbed and debearded

¾ cup dry white wine

2 tablespoons olive oil

2 shallots, finely chopped

1 garlic clove, finely chopped

a scant cup heavy cream

6 oz. (around 4 cups) young leaf spinach

15 basil leaves, shredded

Serves 4

Preparation time: 30 minutes

Cooking time: 20 minutes

crab & rice soup

1 Cut the crabmeat into ½-inch pieces. Heat the oil in a heavy pot. Add the crabmeat and cook over a low heat until lightly browned. Add the onion and cook over medium heat, stirring constantly, for 5 minutes. Add the tomatoes, paprika, salt, and boiling water. Lower the heat, cover, and cook for about 45 minutes.

2 Meanwhile, pound the garlic cloves in a mortar with a pinch of salt and the parsley. Add the saffron strands and 2 tablespoons of the simmering stock. Stir the mixture well.

3 Add the garlic mixture and rice to the pot. Simmer, partially covered, for 20 minutes, or until the rice is tender. Turn off the heat and leave the soup to rest for 2–3 minutes. Stir, and adjust the seasoning, if necessary. Pour the soup into a warmed tureen and serve hot with croûtons.

1 lb. crabmeat

¼ cup olive oil

1 onion, chopped

½ lb. (around ¾ cup) peeled (see page 9) and chopped tomatoes

1 teaspoon paprika

½ teaspoon salt

2 quarts boiling water

2 garlic cloves

2 parsley sprigs

3 saffron strands

1⅓ cups long-grain white rice

salt

croûtons, to garnish (see page 9)

Serves 6
Preparation time: 15 minutes
Cooking time: 1¼ hours

■ If fresh crab is not available, use the frozen and defrosted crabmeat rather than canned, as it has a much better flavor.

crab soup

1 quart Chicken Stock (see page 7)

1-inch piece fresh ginger, peeled and very finely chopped

2 ripe tomatoes, peeled (see page 9), seeded, and very finely chopped

½ small red or green chile, seeded and very finely chopped

2 tablespoons rice wine or dry sherry

1 tablespoon rice wine vinegar, white wine vinegar, or cider vinegar

½ teaspoon sugar

1 tablespoon cornstarch

5 oz. (around ¾ cup) crabmeat, defrosted and drained thoroughly, if frozen

salt and pepper

2 scallions, finely sliced, to garnish

Serves 4–6

Preparation time: 10 minutes

Cooking time: about 20 minutes

1 Pour the stock into a large pot. Add the ginger, tomatoes, chile, rice wine or sherry, vinegar, and sugar. Bring to a boil, cover the pan, and simmer for about 10 minutes to allow the flavors to mingle and mellow.

2 Blend the cornstarch to a paste with a little cold water, then pour it into the soup and stir to blend. Simmer, stirring, for 1–2 minutes until the soup thickens.

3 Add the crabmeat, stir gently to mix, then heat through for 2–3 minutes. Taste, and add salt and pepper, if necessary. Serve piping hot, sprinkled with the sliced scallions.

- quick & easy carrot soup
- carrot & parsnip soup
- celery, carrot & apple soup
- sweet potato soup
- curried parsnip soup
- cream of celeriac soup with porcini dumplings
- root vegetable soup
- zucchini soup with fresh ginger
- zucchini & mint soup
- jerusalem artichoke soup
- no-fuss cauliflower soup
- curried cream of broccoli soup
- borscht
- mushroom soup with madeira
- garlic & spinach soup with parmesan dumplings
- tomato chowder
- asparagus soup

vegetable soups

quick & easy carrot soup

½ stick (¼ cup) butter

1 onion, chopped

1 lb. (around 3 cups) sliced carrots

2 turnips, diced

1 quart water

2½ cups Vegetable Stock (see page 8)

½ lb. (around 2 cups) sliced potatoes

pinch of sugar

3 tablespoons heavy cream (optional)

salt and pepper

Serves 6–8
Preparation time: 15 minutes
Cooking time: 30–35 minutes

1 Melt the butter in a large pot. Add the onion and cook over a moderate heat, stirring frequently, for 5 minutes, until soft, but not golden. Add the carrots and turnips, and cook, stirring constantly, for 1 minute. Pour in the water and stock. Stir, then add the potatoes and sugar, and season with salt and pepper to taste. Bring to a boil, then lower the heat, cover, and simmer for 25–30 minutes. Cool slightly.

2 Purée the soup in a blender or food processor, in batches, if necessary, until smooth. Transfer the puréed soup to a clean pot.

3 Stir well and heat thoroughly without boiling. Taste, and season with more salt and pepper, if necessary. Just before serving, stir in the cream, if you like.

carrot & parsnip soup

½ lb. (around 1 cup) chopped parsnips

½ lb. (around 1½ cups) chopped carrots

1 onion, chopped

2½ cups Chicken Stock (see page 7)

salt and pepper

plain yogurt, to garnish

Serves 4
Preparation time: 15 minutes
Cooking time: about 30 minutes

1 Put the parsnips, carrots, and onion in a large pot with the stock, and season with salt and pepper to taste. Bring to a boil, cover, and simmer for 20 minutes, or until the vegetables are tender.

2 Remove from the heat and allow to cool slightly, then purée in a food processor or blender until smooth, or press through a fine strainer.

3 Return the soup to the cleaned pot and reheat. Serve hot in individual warmed soup bowls, garnished with a swirl of yogurt.

celery, carrot & apple soup

½ stick (¼ cup) unsalted butter

1 lb. (5–5½ cups) chopped celery

1 lb. (3 cups) chopped carrots

1 lb. (1½ cups) peeled, cored, and coarsely chopped eating apples

5 cups Vegetable Stock (see page 8)

1 teaspoon paprika

pinch of cayenne pepper

1 tablespoon chopped basil leaves

1 bay leaf

1 teaspoon grated fresh ginger

salt and freshly ground white pepper

To Garnish:

chopped celery leaves

paprika

Serves 6
Preparation time: 15 minutes
Cooking time: 1 hour

1 Melt the butter in a large pot. Add the celery, carrots, and apples, cover with a tight-fitting lid, and cook over low heat, stirring occasionally, for 15 minutes.

2 Add the stock, paprika, cayenne pepper, basil leaves, bay leaf, and ginger. Bring to a boil, lower the heat, partially cover, and simmer for 40–45 minutes, or until the vegetables and apples are very soft.

3 Purée the soup in a blender or food processor, in batches, if necessary, until smooth. Strain the soup through a strainer back into the clean pot. Season with salt and pepper to taste. Reheat the soup and serve it in warmed bowls, garnished with chopped celery leaves and a light sprinkling of paprika.

sweet potato soup

1 Cook the bacon in a heavy frying pan over low heat until the fat runs, then increase the heat and fry over medium heat until very crisp. Using tongs, transfer the bacon to paper towels to drain.

2 Discard all but 1 tablespoon of bacon fat from the pan. Add the butter. Add the onion, carrots, celery, and bay leaf, and fry over a low heat, stirring frequently, for 5–8 minutes. Transfer the mixture to a pot. Add the sweet potatoes, potatoes, stock, water, and white wine. Bring the mixture to a boil, then lower the heat, cover, and simmer for about 35–40 minutes, or until the vegetables are very tender. Remove and discard the bay leaf.

3 Purée the mixture in a blender or food processor, in batches, if necessary, until smooth. Transfer the soup to a clean pot. Add the nutmeg, white pepper, and salt to taste. Place the pot over a moderate heat and stir until the soup is hot. Serve the soup in warmed bowls. Crumble a little of the reserved bacon over each portion as a garnish.

12 slices bacon

2 tablespoons butter

1 onion, chopped

2 carrots, sliced

2 celery stalks, chopped

1 bay leaf

1½ lb. (around 5½–6 cups) sliced sweet potatoes

½ lb. (around 2 cups) sliced potatoes

5 cups Chicken Stock (see page 7)

⅔ cup water

½ cup dry white wine

¼ teaspoon grated nutmeg

¼ teaspoon freshly ground white pepper

salt

Serves 6–8

Preparation time: 15 minutes

Cooking time: 50 minutes

curried parsnip soup

½ stick (¼ cup) butter

1 teaspoon curry powder

2 large onions, chopped

1½ lb. (around 3 cups) chopped parsnips

2½ cups Chicken Stock (see page 7)

1¼ cups milk

⅔ cup light cream

salt and freshly ground white pepper

1 red apple, cored, diced, and tossed in lemon juice, to garnish

Serves 6–8
Preparation time: 10 minutes
Cooking time: 40–45 minutes

1 Melt the butter in a large pot. Stir in the curry powder and cook, stirring constantly, for 2 minutes. Add the onions and parsnips and cook over a low heat, stirring occasionally, for 5 minutes. Add the stock, and season with salt and pepper to taste.

2 Bring to a boil and cook for 25–30 minutes, or until the vegetables are tender. Cool slightly.

3 Purée the soup in a blender or food processor, or rub through a strainer until smooth. Return to the pot and add the milk and cream. Heat gently, stirring constantly. Check the seasoning and serve immediately, garnished with diced apple.

cream of celeriac soup with porcini dumplings

½ stick (¼ cup) butter

2 shallots or 1 onion, chopped

1 garlic clove, crushed

1 lb. (around 4 cups) diced celeriac (celery root)

1 quart Chicken or Vegetable Stock (see pages 7 and 8)

1¼ cups light cream or milk

salt and pepper

finely grated Parmesan cheese, to garnish

Porcini Dumplings:

¼ oz. dried porcini mushrooms

2 tablespoons butter

1 shallot, very finely chopped

¾ cup ricotta cheese

½ cup finely grated Parmesan cheese

2 egg yolks, beaten

2 tablespoons all-purpose flour plus extra for dusting

1 tablespoon chopped parsley

Serves 4–6

Preparation time: 25 minutes plus soaking

Cooking time: 30 minutes

1 To make the dumplings, place the porcini in a small bowl, cover with warm water, and leave to soak for 30 minutes. Drain in a fine strainer, reserving the liquid. Rinse the mushrooms well in cold water, chop finely, and set aside.

2 Melt the butter in a small pan over low heat. Add the shallot and cook for 5–6 minutes, or until softened, but not colored. Spoon into a bowl, add the mushrooms, ricotta, Parmesan, egg yolks, flour, and parsley, and mix to form a soft dough. Season to taste. Cover and chill for 30–60 minutes. With lightly floured hands, form the dough into 30 small balls, then roll them in flour and place on a tray.

3 To make the soup, melt the butter in a pot over low heat. Add the shallots or onion and garlic, and cook, stirring frequently, for 5 minutes, until softened, but not colored. Add the celeriac, cover, and cook for 5–10 minutes, until the celeriac begins to soften. Add the stock and the reserved mushroom liquid. Bring to a boil, reduce the heat, and simmer for 10–15 minutes.

4 Purée the soup in a blender or food processor until smooth. Return the soup to the pot, stir in the cream or milk, and season to taste. Reheat gently.

5 Bring a pot of salted water to a boil. Add the dumplings and simmer for 3–4 minutes. Drain well, and add to the soup just before serving. Serve the soup sprinkled with grated Parmesan cheese.

root vegetable soup

1 Put all the diced vegetables and garlic into a 2-gallon pot. Cover with the water and add the salt and butter. For the bouquet garni, tie the herbs, peppercorns, and celery seeds loosely in cheesecloth, and add to the pot. Bring to a boil, lower the heat, and simmer for about 40 minutes, until all the vegetables are tender.

2 Let cool slightly. Purée the mixture in a blender or food processor, in batches, and transfer the soup to a clean pot.

3 Reheat and serve with one or all of the suggested garnishes, if you like. The soup can be thinned, if necessary, with water, stock, light cream, or tomato juice.

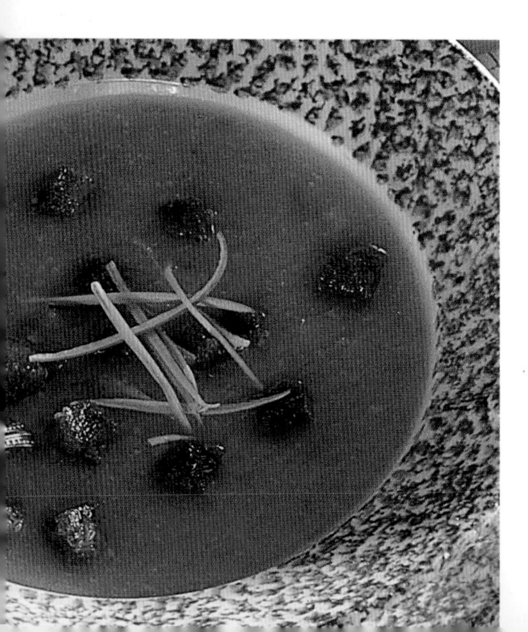

1 lb. (4 cups) roughly diced potatoes

1 lb. (3 cups) roughly diced carrots

1 lb. (2½–3 cups) roughly diced rutabaga

1 lb. (2 cups) roughly diced parsnips

1 lb. (around 2–2½ cups) roughly diced onions

1 lb. (4 cups) roughly diced celeriac (celery root)

2 large garlic cloves, crushed

2½ quarts water

2 teaspoons salt

1 stick (½ cup) butter

Bouquet Garni:

2 bay leaves

1 thyme sprig

1 marjoram sprig

1 oregano sprig

2 teaspoons peppercorns

1 teaspoon celery seeds

Optional Garnishes:

4 batches croûtons (see page 9) and 1 bunch scallions, finely sliced

or 2 bunches chives, finely snipped and 2 tablespoons chopped parsley

or ⅔ cup heavy cream

Serves 8–12

Preparation time: 45 minutes

Cooking time: 35–40 minutes

1 Use a vegetable peeler to pare 1 zucchini lengthwise into thin ribbons. Set these aside for the garnish. Thickly slice the remaining zucchini and place in a colander. Sprinkle with salt and leave to stand for 10–15 minutes. Rinse in cold water, drain thoroughly, and pat dry with paper towels.

2 Melt the butter in a large pot. Add the onions and cook over medium heat, stirring frequently, for 5 minutes, until soft, but not golden. Add the zucchini and cook, stirring frequently, for 5 minutes. Add the stock, ginger, and nutmeg, with pepper to taste. Bring to a boil and add the potatoes. Lower the heat, partially cover, and simmer for 40–45 minutes, or until the vegetables are very soft.

3 Purée the soup in a blender or food processor, in batches, until smooth. Transfer to a clean pot. Reheat gently and serve in warmed soup bowls. Garnish each portion with a swirl of cream, if you like, and a few of the reserved zucchini ribbons, sprinkled with a little coarsely ground black pepper.

CHICKEN BOUILLON 4 TE-SP
GARLIC · 2 TB-SP

3 lb. small zucchini

½ stick (¼ cup) butter

1 cup chopped onions

1 quart Vegetable Stock (see page 8)

1 tablespoon grated fresh ginger

pinch of grated nutmeg

¾ lb. (around 3 cups) chopped potatoes

salt and pepper

coarsely ground black pepper, to serve

⅔ cup light cream, to garnish (optional)

Serves 6

Preparation time: 15 minutes

Cooking time: 55 minutes

zucchini soup with fresh ginger

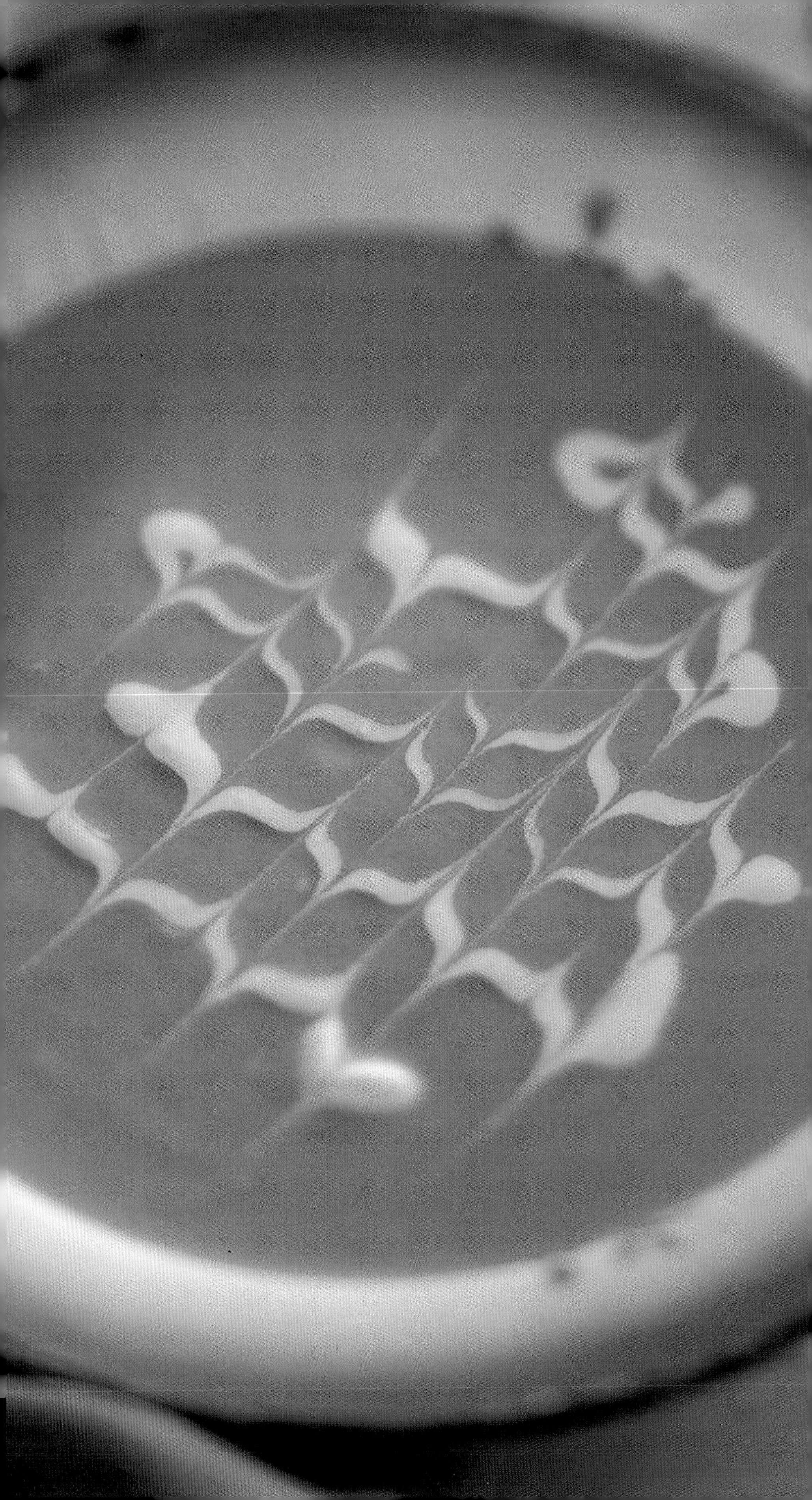

zucchini & mint soup

½ stick (¼ cup) butter

1 small onion, chopped

1–2 garlic cloves, crushed

1½ lb. (around 5 cups) diced zucchini

finely grated zest of 1 lemon

2½ cups Chicken Stock (see page 7) or water

2–3 tablespoons chopped mint

2 egg yolks

½ cup heavy cream

salt and pepper

light cream, to garnish

Serves 4
Preparation time: 20 minutes
Cooking time: 25 minutes

1 Melt the butter in a pot over low heat. Add the onion and garlic and cook, stirring frequently, for 5–6 minutes, until the onion has softened. Stir in the zucchini and lemon zest, and cook for a further 5–10 minutes, until tender.

2 Add the stock or water and mint, bring to a boil, then simmer for 5 minutes. Purée the soup in a blender or food processor until smooth, then strain through a strainer.

3 Just before serving, reheat the soup to just below boiling point. Mix together the egg yolks and cream in a small bowl, and whisk in a ladleful of the hot soup. Whisk this mixture back into the pot of soup, but do not allow the soup to boil or it will curdle. Season to taste with salt and pepper, and serve in warmed individual bowls. To garnish, drizzle several lines of light cream across the surface of the soup. Drag a toothpick through the lines to give a feathered effect.

jerusalem artichoke soup

1 Place the lemon juice in a large bowl and add plenty of cold water. Peel the artichokes; set aside 2 and cut the rest into ¾-inch pieces. Drop the artichokes into the lemon water as you prepare them to prevent discoloration.

2 Melt the butter in a large, heavy pot. Add the onion, garlic, celery, thyme, and lemon zest, and cook over a low heat for 6–8 minutes, until softened, but not colored. Drain the chopped artichokes and add to the pot, with the stock. Season to taste with salt and pepper, bring to a boil, reduce the heat, and simmer for about 15 minutes, or until the artichokes are tender.

3 To prepare the artichoke crisps, drain the 2 whole artichokes, slice thinly, and dry well on paper towels. Heat some oil in a deep pot to 350–375°F, or until a cube of bread browns in 30 seconds. Fry the artichoke slices in batches, until crisp and golden. Drain them well on paper towels.

4 Purée the soup in a blender or food processor, in batches, if necessary. Strain through a strainer and return to the pot. Add the cream or milk, and a little water if too thick, season to taste with salt and pepper, and reheat gently. Stir in the finely grated Parmesan and serve sprinkled with the artichoke crisps.

finely grated zest and juice of 1 small lemon

1¼ lb. Jerusalem artichokes

½ stick (¼ cup) butter

1 onion, chopped

1 garlic clove, crushed

1 celery stalk, chopped

½ teaspoon lemon thyme leaves

1 quart Chicken or Vegetable Stock (see pages 7 and 8)

oil, for frying

¾ cup light cream or milk

3 tablespoons finely grated Parmesan cheese

salt and pepper

Serves 4

Preparation time: 25 minutes

Cooking time: 30 minutes

Instead of making the Jerusalem artichoke crisps, toast ½ cup of hazelnuts, leave to cool, then coarsely grind or chop them. Sprinkle over the soup to serve.

no-fuss cauliflower soup

½ stick (¼ cup) butter

1 onion, chopped

1 celery stalk, chopped

1 large cauliflower, about 1½ lb., cut into small florets

1 quart Vegetable Stock (see page 8)

3 cups milk

1 teaspoon grated nutmeg

1 tablespoon cornstarch

salt and freshly ground white pepper

finely chopped parsley, to garnish

Serves 6–8
Preparation time: 15 minutes
Cooking time: 35 minutes

1 Melt the butter in a large pot. Add the onion, celery, and cauliflower, cover, and cook over medium heat, stirring frequently, for 5–8 minutes. Stir in the stock with 2 cups of the milk. Bring to a boil, then lower the heat, cover, and simmer for 25 minutes.

2 Purée the soup in a blender or food processor, in batches, until smooth. Pour the soup into a clean pot. Stir in half of the remaining milk. Season with salt and pepper to taste, and stir in the nutmeg.

3 In a small bowl, mix the cornstarch with the remaining milk to a smooth paste, and add it to the soup. Bring to a boil, stirring constantly. Lower the heat and simmer for 2 minutes. Serve immediately in warmed soup bowls. Garnish each portion with a sprinkling of finely chopped parsley.

curried cream of broccoli soup

1 Strip off all the tough stems and leaves from the broccoli. Cut off the stalks, peel them, and cut them into 1-inch pieces. Break the florets into very small pieces, and set them aside.

2 Melt the butter in a large pot. Add the onion and broccoli stalks, cover, and cook over medium heat, stirring frequently, for 5 minutes. Add the reserved florets, potato, curry powder, and stock. Bring to a boil. Partially cover and cook for 5 minutes. Using a slotted spoon, remove 6 or more broccoli florets for the garnish, if you like, and set aside. Season well with salt and pepper. Continue to cook over medium heat for 20 minutes, or until all the vegetables are soft.

3 Purée the soup in a blender or food processor, in batches, if necessary, until smooth. Pour the soup into a clean pot. Add the cream, and heat thoroughly without allowing the soup to boil. Serve in warmed soup bowls, garnishing each portion with the reserved florets, if using.

2 lb. (2 large bunches) broccoli

½ stick (¼ cup) butter

1 onion, chopped

1 large potato, quartered

1 tablespoon medium-hot curry powder

1½ quarts Vegetable Stock (see page 8)

⅔ cup light cream

salt and pepper

Serves 6

Preparation time: 10–15 minutes

Cooking time: 25 minutes

borscht

1 Place the beets in a pot, cover with plenty of cold water, and add 1 tablespoon salt. Bring to a boil, lower the heat, cover, and simmer steadily for 35–45 minutes. Drain, discarding the liquid, then rinse the beets under cold water, dry with paper towels, and slip off the skins.

2 Grate the beets into a large pot. Add the tomatoes, beef stock, cabbage, 2 teaspoons salt, the bay leaf, caraway seeds, peppercorns, vinegar, and sugar. Stir well. Bring to a boil, lower the heat, cover the pan, and simmer gently for about 1½ hours.

3 Remove and discard the bay leaf. Add the potatoes to the soup and continue simmering until they are tender, but not too soft. Serve the soup hot, in warmed soup bowls, and garnish each portion with a teaspoon of sour cream, if using.

4 raw beets

4 tomatoes, peeled (see page 9) and chopped

5 cups Beef Stock (see page 7)

3 large cabbage leaves, coarsely shredded

1 bay leaf

½ teaspoon caraway seeds

6 black peppercorns, crushed

5 tablespoons red wine vinegar

2 tablespoons sugar

6 small potatoes

salt

6 teaspoons sour cream, to garnish (optional)

Serves 6

Preparation time: 15 minutes

Cooking time: about 3 hours

mushroom soup with madeira

¾ stick (⅓ cup) butter

1 large onion, finely chopped

1 lb. (5–6 cups) finely chopped mushrooms

¼ cup all-purpose flour

1 quart Chicken Stock (see page 7)

½ cup dry Madeira wine

⅔ cup heavy cream

salt and pepper

chopped parsley, to garnish

Serves 4–6
Preparation time: 5 minutes
Cooking time: 40 minutes

1 Melt the butter in a large pot. Add the onion and cook over low heat, stirring frequently, for 20 minutes, or until evenly browned. Add the mushrooms and cook for 2 minutes.

2 Stir in the flour and cook for 1 minute. Gradually stir in the stock, then season with salt and pepper to taste. Bring to a boil, cover, and simmer for 10 minutes.

3 Stir in the Madeira and cream and heat through gently. Serve immediately, garnished with parsley.

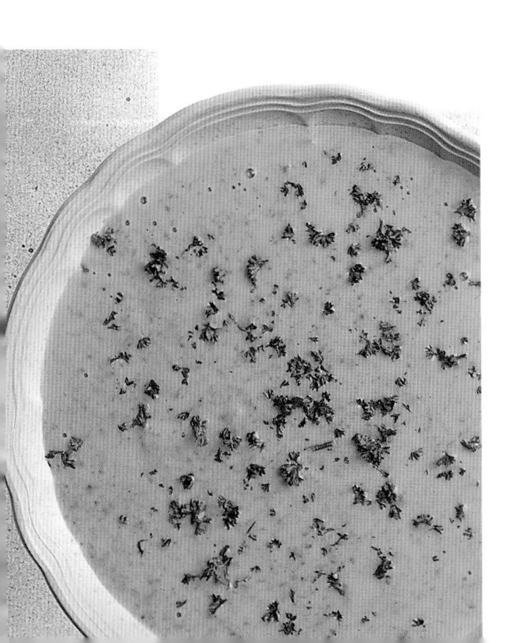

garlic & spinach soup with parmesan dumplings

5 tablespoons olive oil

2 small heads garlic, peeled

2 medium onions, sliced

1 lb. (around 4 small-to-medium) potatoes, diced

1 bay leaf

1 thyme sprig

pinch of saffron threads

5 cups Chicken or Vegetable Stock (see pages 7 and 8)

2½ cups milk

½ lb. (about 3 large handfuls) fresh spinach, tough stems removed, finely shredded

salt and pepper

coarsely ground black peppercorns, for serving

Parmesan Dumplings:

¾ cup ricotta cheese

2 tablespoons butter, softened

½ cup finely grated Parmesan cheese

1 teaspoon finely grated lemon zest

2 tablespoons all-purpose flour plus extra for rolling

2 egg yolks, beaten

freshly grated nutmeg

Serves 4–6
Preparation time: 30 minutes
Cooking time: 55 minutes

1 To make the Parmesan dumplings, place all the ingredients in a bowl and mix to form a firm paste. Season to taste with salt, pepper, and nutmeg. Cover and chill in the refrigerator for 30–60 minutes. With lightly floured hands, form the mixture into 24 small balls, roll in flour, and place on a tray.

2 To make the soup, heat the oil in a pot. Add the garlic and onions, and cook over low heat for 5 minutes, until softened, but not colored. Cover with a tight-fitting lid and cook for 30–35 minutes, until very soft, but do not allow the garlic or onions to color.

3 Add the potatoes, bay leaf, thyme, saffron, stock, and milk, and season to taste with salt and pepper. Bring to a boil, reduce the heat, and simmer for 20–30 minutes. Add the spinach and cook for 1–2 minutes, until it has wilted.

4 Purée the soup in a blender or food processor, in batches, if necessary. Strain through a strainer into a clean pot and reheat. Bring a small pot of lightly salted water to a boil and drop in the dumplings. Cook for 3–4 minutes, drain well, and add some to each serving of soup. Serve sprinkled with coarsely ground black peppercorns.

tomato chowder

1 Combine all the ingredients, except the cheese, in a large pot. Stir well. Bring to a boil over medium heat, stirring constantly, then lower the heat and simmer for 3 minutes.

2 Ladle the soup into warmed ovenproof bowls, sprinkle with the cheese, and place under a preheated hot broiler for 3–5 minutes, or until the cheese is bubbling. Serve the chowder immediately.

a 10 oz. can condensed tomato soup

a 14 oz. can tomato purée

an 11 oz. can corn, drained

1 tablespoon Worcestershire sauce

3–6 drops Tabasco sauce

1 teaspoon chopped oregano

½ teaspoon sugar

1 cup shredded Cheddar cheese

Serves 4–6

Preparation time: 5 minutes

Cooking time: about 10 minutes

asparagus soup

20 asparagus spears

1 quart Chicken Stock (see page 7)

2 cups peas or 4 large handfuls spinach, chopped

1 teaspoon sugar

2 tablespoons butter

¼ cup all-purpose flour

⅔ cup milk

6 tablespoons heavy cream

salt and pepper

Serves 6

Preparation time: 15 minutes

Cooking time: 30 minutes

1 Discard all but the top 2½–3½ inches of the asparagus spears, as the lower part may make the soup bitter. Cut the remainder into 1-inch lengths. Reserve a few ½-inch tips for garnishing, and cook these separately for 10 minutes in a little boiling, salted water.

2 Bring the stock to a boil. Add the asparagus, peas or spinach, and sugar, and season to taste with salt and pepper. Bring back to a boil, lower the heat, and simmer until the vegetables are tender. Cool slightly, then blend the vegetables and stock in a food processor, or press the soup through a strainer.

3 Melt the butter in the clean pot, stir in the flour and add the asparagus purée. Bring to a boil, stirring and adding the milk. Ladle into a warmed tureen or individual soup bowls. Stir in the cream, add a few asparagus tips to garnish, and serve immediately.

chilled soups

vichyssoise

1 Melt the butter in a pot. Add the onions and cook over low heat, stirring frequently, for 10 minutes, until softened, but not browned.

2 Add the leeks and potatoes and toss well. Stir in the stock, add the bouquet garni, and season with salt and pepper to taste. Bring to a boil, cover, and simmer, stirring occasionally, for 30–40 minutes. Remove and discard the bouquet garni, and cool slightly.

3 Purée the soup in a blender or food processor until smooth. Pour into a soup tureen and leave until cool. Stir in the cream. Chill for 3–4 hours. Garnish with chives and croûtons just before serving.

½ stick (¼ cup) butter

2 large onions, chopped

4 large leeks, white parts only, sliced

4 large potatoes, diced

5 cups Chicken Stock (see page 7)

1 bouquet garni

⅔ cup heavy cream

salt and freshly ground white pepper

To Garnish:

2 tablespoons snipped chives

croûtons (see page 9)

Serves 6

Preparation time: 15 minutes plus chilling

Cooking time: 45–50 minutes

mint, cucumber & green pea soup

½ stick (¼ cup) butter

1 lb. cucumbers, peeled, seeded, and cut into ½-inch pieces (around 2¾ cups)

2 cups fresh or frozen peas, defrosted

pinch of sugar

¼ teaspoon white pepper

3 tablespoons finely chopped mint

5 cups Chicken or Vegetable Stock (see pages 7 and 8)

1 generous cup chopped potatoes

salt

⅔ cup heavy cream, chilled

Serves 6
Preparation time: 15 minutes plus chilling
Cooking time: 25–30 minutes

1 Melt the butter in a large pot. Add the cucumber and cook over medium heat, stirring occasionally, for 5 minutes. Add the peas, sugar, pepper, and 2 tablespoons of the mint. Pour in the stock. Bring to a boil, then add the potatoes. Lower the heat, partially cover, and simmer gently for about 20 minutes, or until the potatoes are tender.

2 Purée the soup in a blender or food processor, in batches, if necessary, until smooth. Transfer the soup to a bowl. Season with salt to taste. Cool, cover the bowl tightly, and chill in the refrigerator for at least 3 hours.

3 Just before serving, fold in the chilled cream. Serve in chilled bowls, garnishing each portion with a little of the remaining mint, if you like.

■ This soup is equally delicious served hot. After blending to a purée, return the soup to a clean pot, add the cream, and reheat gently without boiling. Serve in warmed bowls, garnishing each portion with a little chopped mint.

chilled cucumber & yellow pepper soup

1 Cut off a third of 1 cucumber. Dice finely and set aside for the garnish. Roughly chop the remaining cucumber.

2 Place the chopped cucumber and garlic in a blender or food processor and purée until very smooth. Pour into a bowl and stir in the yogurt. Add enough iced water to make a smooth soup. Season to taste with salt and pepper. Stir in the mint, cover, and chill thoroughly.

3 Chop finely 1 yellow pepper, mix with the reserved cucumber, and set aside for the garnish. Chop the remaining pepper and place in a small saucepan with the lime or lemon juice, sugar, 6 tablespoons of the water, and a pinch of cayenne. Bring to a boil, reduce the heat, and simmer for 10–15 minutes, until the pepper is soft and the liquid has reduced. Remove from the heat and purée in a blender or food processor. Strain the purée through a strainer into a bowl. Let cool, cover, and chill in the refrigerator.

4 Ladle the soup into individual bowls. Sprinkle with the diced pepper and cucumber, and drizzle the yellow pepper purée over it.

2 cucumbers, peeled and seeded

1 garlic clove, crushed

1 cup plain yogurt

½ cup iced water

¼ cup chopped mint

2 yellow bell peppers, cored and seeded

2 tablespoons lime or lemon juice

1 tablespoon sugar

cayenne pepper

salt and pepper

Serves 4–6

Preparation time: 30 minutes plus chilling

Cooking time: 10–15 minutes

■ As a variation, substitute fresh dill for the mint and garnish the soup with fresh crabmeat.

simple chilled potato chowder

1 Melt the butter in a large pot. Add the potatoes and onions, and cook, stirring frequently, for 10 minutes, or until the onions are softened slightly.

2 Add the mushroom soup, milk, and mustard, and season with salt and pepper to taste. Stir well. Heat gently until the soup begins to simmer. Pour the soup into a bowl and let cool. Cover the bowl tightly and chill the chowder in the refrigerator for at least 3 hours.

3 Serve in chilled bowls, garnishing each portion with a little cottage cheese, if using, a few snipped chives, and a light dusting of paprika.

2 tablespoons butter

5 potatoes, diced

3 onions, sliced

a 15 oz. can cream of mushroom soup

1 quart milk

1 teaspoon English mustard

salt and pepper

To Garnish:

2 tablespoons cottage cheese (optional)

a few snipped chives

paprika

Serves 6

Preparation time: 10 minutes plus chilling

Cooking time: about 20 minutes

chilled shrimp & pea soup

1½ lb. fresh young peas in the pod or 2 cups frozen peas, defrosted

½ lb. cooked small shrimp in their shells

1 onion, chopped

1 garlic clove, crushed

2½ cups Chicken Stock (see page 7) or water

pinch of grated nutmeg

⅔ cup dry white wine (optional)

⅔ cup sour cream

1 tablespoon lemon juice

salt and pepper

To Serve:

sour cream (optional)

4 teaspoons salmon roe (optional)

2 tablespoons snipped chives

French bread (optional)

Serves 4
Preparation time: 30 minutes plus chilling
Cooking time: 30 minutes

1 Shell the peas if using fresh, reserving the pods. Peel the shrimp, reserving the shells and refrigerate. Place the shrimp shells and pea pods, if available, in a large pot with the onion, garlic, and stock. Bring to a boil, reduce the heat, and simmer gently for 15 minutes.

2 Strain the stock into a clean pot, add the peas, and season with salt, pepper, and nutmeg. Bring back to a boil, reduce the heat, and simmer until the peas are tender. Purée the mixture in a blender or food processor until smooth. Pour into a bowl, adjust the seasoning to taste, stir in the wine, if using, sour cream, and lemon juice. Cool, cover the bowl, and chill thoroughly.

3 Pour the soup into individual bowls and divide the shrimp among them. Add a spoonful of sour cream and some salmon roe, if using. Sprinkle with chives and serve with French bread, if you like.

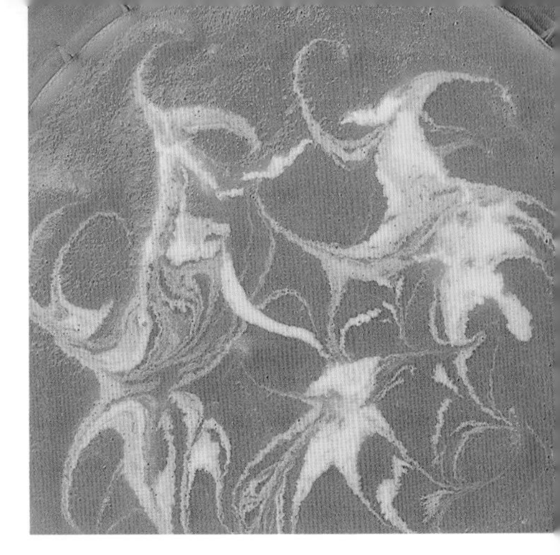

carrot & orange soup

1 Melt the butter in a large pot. Add the carrots and onion, and cook over low heat, stirring frequently, for 10 minutes, without browning.

2 Add the stock, sugar, and salt and pepper to taste. Bring to a boil, cover, and simmer for 1 hour, or until the carrots are tender. Let cool slightly.

3 Strain the soup or purée it in a blender or food processor, until smooth. Pour into a soup tureen and stir in the orange zest and juice. Let cool, then cover tightly and chill in the refrigerator for several hours. Just before serving, stir in the cream.

2 tablespoons butter

3 cups sliced carrots

1 onion, chopped

1 quart Chicken Stock (see page 7)

pinch of sugar

grated zest of 1 orange

juice of 4 oranges

⅔ cup light cream, chilled

salt and pepper

Serves 6

Preparation time: 15 minutes plus chilling

Cooking time: 1¼ hours

Make sure that the oranges are at room temperature before squeezing them, because this increases the quantity of juice they yield.

no-cook gazpacho

2 garlic cloves, roughly chopped

¼ teaspoon salt

3 thick slices white bread, crusts removed

2 lb. tomatoes, peeled (see page 9) and coarsely chopped (around 3 cups)

2 onions, coarsely chopped

½ large cucumber, peeled, seeded, and coarsely chopped

2 large green peppers, cored, seeded, and coarsely chopped

5 tablespoons olive oil

¼ cup white wine vinegar

1 quart water

pepper

croûtons (optional, see page 9), to garnish

Serves 6

Preparation time: 10–15 minutes plus chilling

1 Combine the garlic and salt in a mortar and pound with a pestle until smooth. Or instead, place the garlic and salt on a board, and crush the garlic with the flat blade of a large knife. Place the bread in a bowl, and cover with cold water. Soak for 5 seconds, then drain the bread, squeezing out the moisture.

2 Set aside a quarter of the tomatoes, onions, cucumber, and peppers for the garnish. Place the remaining vegetables in a blender or food processor. Add the garlic paste, bread, and oil, and blend the mixture until it is very smooth. Pour the mixture into a bowl and stir in the vinegar and water, with pepper to taste. Cover tightly and chill in the refrigerator for at least 3 hours.

3 Chop the reserved vegetables finely and place them in small bowls. Serve the soup very cold, in chilled individual bowls. Add a selection of the vegetable accompaniments to the soup, as you like, and offer the remainder in their small bowls so that they can be added to people's individual tastes. Croûtons may also be served.

white gazpacho

4 slices day-old white bread, crusts removed

½ cup coarsely chopped blanched almonds

1–2 garlic cloves, chopped

½ cup extra-virgin olive oil

2–3 tablespoons sherry or white wine vinegar

1 quart ice water

salt

½ lb. (1½ cups) white seedless grapes, cut in half, to garnish

Serves 4

Preparation time: 10–15 minutes plus chilling

1 Place the bread in a bowl, cover with cold water, and set aside to soak for 5 minutes. Squeeze the water out of the bread.

2 Place the almonds and garlic in a blender or food processor, then blend until very finely ground and almost paste-like. With the motor running, gradually add the bread and blend until smooth. Then gradually add the oil in a thin stream. When all the oil has been incorporated, add the vinegar, scraping the mixture down the sides of the bowl, if necessary. Pour in 1¼ cups of the ice water and blend briefly to mix.

3 Strain through a strainer into a large bowl, pressing with the back of a ladle to extract as much liquid as possible. Stir in more ice water to make a thin soup, and season to taste with salt. Cover tightly and chill thoroughly.

4 Just before serving, stir the soup well as it may have separated slightly. Ladle the soup into chilled individual bowls and garnish with a few grape halves.

chilled tomato soup

2 tablespoons olive oil

2 tablespoons butter

1 large onion, chopped

1 garlic clove, chopped

1½–2 lb. tomatoes, peeled (see page 9) and coarsely chopped (around 2–3 cups)

1 quart Chicken Stock (see page 7)

1 teaspoon chopped oregano

1½ teaspoons sugar

¼ teaspoon celery salt

pinch of grated nutmeg

1 tablespoon Worcestershire sauce

⅔ cup sour cream

salt and pepper

To Garnish:

6 Spanish olives

chopped parsley (optional)

Serves 6

Preparation time: 20–25 minutes plus chilling

Cooking time: 50–55 minutes

1 Heat the olive oil and butter in a heavy pot. Add the onion and garlic, and cook over low heat, stirring frequently, for 3–5 minutes, or until softened, but not golden. Add the tomatoes and cook, stirring frequently, for 3 minutes.

2 Add the stock, oregano, sugar, celery salt, nutmeg, and Worcestershire sauce, and season with salt and pepper to taste. Stir well and bring to a boil. Lower the heat, partially cover, and simmer for 45 minutes. Cool slightly.

3 Purée the soup in a blender or food processor, then transfer to a bowl. Stir in the sour cream and allow the soup to cool completely, then cover the bowl tightly and chill in the refrigerator for at least 3 hours.

4 Meanwhile, place one Spanish olive per cube in 6 cubes of an ice tray, and top up with cold water. Freeze until solid. Serve the soup in chilled bowls, with an olive-filled ice cube on each serving. Garnish with parsley, if you like.

tomato soup with basil

1 Melt the butter in a large pot. Add the onion and cook over low heat, stirring frequently, for 5 minutes, until softened, but not colored. Add the tomatoes and cook, stirring frequently, for 2 minutes.

2 Add the stock and bring to a boil. Lower the heat, add the sugar, and season with salt and pepper to taste. Simmer over a low heat for 20 minutes.

3 Blend briefly in a blender or food processor, or pass through a medium food mill. Adjust the seasoning, cool, and chill well. About 10 minutes before serving, stir in the chopped basil. Garnish with a swirl of cream and a sprinkling of chives.

½ stick (¼ cup) butter

1 large mild onion, chopped

1½ lb. tomatoes, peeled (see page 9) and chopped (around 2¼ cups)

2½ cups hot Chicken Stock (see page 7)

pinch of sugar

3 tablespoons chopped basil

salt and pepper

To Garnish:

1 tablespoon light cream

1 tablespoon snipped chives

Serves 4

Preparation time: 10 minutes plus chilling

Cooking time: 30 minutes

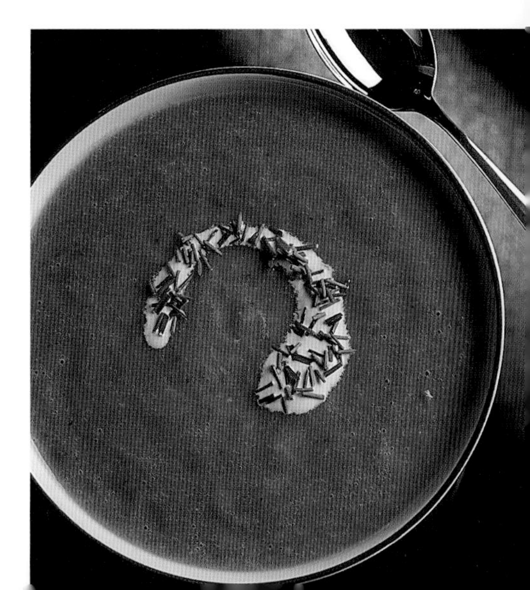

chilled tomato, strawberry & rhubarb soup

1 Put the tomatoes, strawberries, and rhubarb into a 2½-quart stainless steel or enamel pot, and cover with the stock. Add the salt and pepper. Bring to a boil, lower the heat, and simmer for about 10 minutes, or until the fruit is soft.

2 Press through a fine strainer into a bowl. Rub and scrape the pulp through until no more than a tablespoon of debris remains in the strainer. Cool, then chill in the refrigerator, preferably overnight.

3 Serve in chilled bowls with a swirl of cream, if using, and top with peppered strawberry slices with a sprinkling of chives.

2 lb. ripe tomatoes, cut in half and seeded

1½ lb. strawberries, hulled, and cut in half

2 lb. red rhubarb, chopped

2 quarts Chicken Stock (see page 7)

2 teaspoons salt

3–4 teaspoons freshly ground white pepper

1¼ cups heavy cream (optional), to serve

To Garnish:

½ lb. strawberries, hulled, sliced, and lightly peppered

2 tablespoons snipped chives

Serves 12

Preparation time: 30 minutes plus chilling

Cooking time: 10–15 minutes

fig soup with cattucini

16 small figs, preferably black

1 vanilla bean, split lengthwise, or a few drops of vanilla extract

a 2-inch piece of cinnamon stick

2 strips pared orange zest

1 cup water

1⅔ cups red wine

2 tablespoons honey

2 tablespoons fresh lemon juice

To Serve:

cattucini (sweet Italian biscuits)

mascarpone cheese

Serves 4
Preparation time: 15 minutes plus chilling
Cooking time: 15 minutes

1 Set aside 4 of the figs. Place the remaining figs in a large pot with the remaining ingredients. Bring to a boil, lower the heat, and simmer for 2 minutes. Remove from the heat, cover, and leave to steep for 10 minutes.

2 If using a vanilla bean, scrape the seeds into the soup. Discard the vanilla bean, cinnamon stick, and orange zest. Process the soup in a blender or food processor. Strain and return to the pot.

3 Add the reserved figs and bring to a boil. Reduce the heat, cover, and simmer for 5–7 minutes, or until tender, turning the figs over after 2–3 minutes. Transfer the poached figs and soup to a bowl, taste, and add more honey or lemon juice, if needed. Cool, cover, and chill thoroughly.

4 Just before serving, remove the figs with a slotted spoon and cut each fig into wedges. Ladle the soup into chilled bowls and garnish with the fig wedges. Serve with the cattucini biscuits and a spoonful of mascarpone cheese.

apricot, orange & cardamom soup

1 Pare the zest from the oranges, making sure that none of the bitter white pith is attached, and cut into very thin strips. Bring a small saucepan of water to a boil, add the orange zest, and simmer for 2 minutes. Remove from the heat, rinse in cold water and leave to drain.

2 Squeeze the juice from the oranges and pour into a saucepan. Add the sugar and crushed cardamom seeds. Stir over a medium heat until the sugar has dissolved, then set aside to cool.

3 Place the apricots in a blender or food processor with the orange syrup, and blend until smooth. Strain through a strainer into a bowl, cover, and chill thoroughly.

4 Ladle the soup into chilled soup bowls. Top each serving with a spoonful of mascarpone cheese or whipped cream, and decorate with the strips of orange zest.

2 large oranges

½ cup sugar

2 green cardamom pods, seeds removed, and crushed

1½ lb. fresh apricots, cut in half, pitted, and chopped (around 3½–4 cups)

mascarpone cheese or softly whipped cream, to serve

Serves 4

Preparation time: 25 minutes plus chilling

Cooking time: 10 minutes

watermelon & lime soup

1 Using a melon baller, scoop out 20–24 balls of watermelon flesh, cover, and set aside in the refrigerator. Discard the skin from the remaining melon, chop the flesh roughly, and place in a strainer set over a bowl. Push the flesh through the strainer, extracting as much juice as possible. Discard the melon seeds.

2 Place the sugar, water, and lime zest in a small saucepan over low heat. Stir until the sugar has dissolved, bring to a boil, and simmer for 2–3 minutes. Remove from the heat and leave to cool slightly. Pour the lime juice and half of the syrup into the strained melon, and stir to mix. Taste, and add more syrup or lime juice, if necessary. Cover and chill.

3 To serve, ladle the soup into individual bowls or glasses. Add the reserved melon balls, and serve.

a 5-lb. slice watermelon

½ cup sugar

1 cup water

finely grated zest and juice of 1 lime plus extra to taste

sour cream, to serve (optional)

Serves 4

Preparation time: 15 minutes plus chilling

Cooking time: 2–3 minutes

1 Heat the oil in a large pot. Add the onion, cover, and cook over low heat, stirring occasionally, for about 8–10 minutes, until softened, but not colored. Add the fennel and potatoes and cook, stirring occasionally, for a further 10 minutes. Add the garlic, bay leaf, fennel seeds, lemon juice, stock, and apple juice. Season to taste with salt and pepper. Bring to a boil and simmer for approximately 15 minutes, or until the potatoes are very tender.

2 Strain into a bowl through a strainer, reserving the vegetable pulp. Leave to cool. As it cools, surplus oils will rise to the surface of the liquid; skim these off and discard them.

3 Purée the vegetable pulp in a blender or food processor until smooth. Stir the purée into the cooled, skimmed liquid. Cover and chill in the refrigerator, preferably overnight.

4 Before serving, whisk in the chilled cream or yogurt. Add a slice of apple to each serving and sprinkle with a little chopped fennel.

2 tablespoons olive oil

½ cup finely chopped onion

1 fennel bulb, about 10–12 oz., cut into 1-inch cubes

1½–1¾ cups cubed potatoes

1 garlic clove, crushed

1 small bay leaf

1 teaspoon fennel seeds, tied in a piece of cheesecloth

2–3 tablespoons lemon juice

2½ cups Chicken Stock (see page 7)

1¼ cups unsweetened apple juice

salt and pepper

To Garnish:

⅔ cup light cream or a scant cup plain yogurt, chilled

2 Gala (or other eating) apples, peeled, cored, finely sliced, and sprinkled with lemon juice

2 tablespoons chopped fennel fronds

Serves 5–6

Preparation time: 45 minutes plus chilling

Cooking time: 35–40 minutes

chilled fennel & apple soup

index